If God Talked Out Loud...

D0910747

If God Talked Out Loud...

Clyde Lee Herring

Broadman Press
Nashville, Tennessee

© Copyright 1977 ● Broadman Press.

All rights reserved.

4253-25

ISBN: 0-8054-5325-3

Dewey Decimal Classification: 248.83

Subject Heading: CHRISTIAN LIFE//YOUTH

Library of Congress Catalog Card Number: 76-27479

Printed in the United States of America

DEDICATED TO:

All the youth I've pastored in churches, camps, retreats, and Bible conferences. And to those two teens who live in my home whom I'm proud to calls sons: Jeff and Lee.

Introduction

I was thinking about the Lord's Prayer one morning. There is hardly anything more beautiful in all the world . . . and more neglected. It bothered me that we frequently quote Christ's beautiful prayer, and even sing it, with hardly a thought as to its real meaning.

What if God talked out loud? I asked myself. *What if he answered back while someone prayed the Lord's Prayer absentmindedly?*

I turned to my typewriter and began writing what I thought God might say. Thus came the creation of the first chapter of the book, entitled "When You Pray, Say . . ."

The piece was printed first in *event* magazine. It touched the needs of many. Other magazines (*Moody Monthly*, for example) requested the piece. Eventually, about twenty magazines printed the article, including evangelical publications in Mexico, Canada, and Portugal.

Event magazine requested other articles using the same approach. Other subjects needed touching on.

In the meantime, I received letters from all over the country relating how people were using the first article.

Some used it on radio programs on the West Coast, here in Tulsa, and in the deep South. Others had created a drama with it. The "voice of God" was heard offstage, while the pray-er was placed in a spotlight. The play was used on retreats, in worship services, and at fellowships.

Still others, looking for fresh ways to use their puppet ministry, made use of it as a script for their own skits.

I'm deeply grateful to Linda Lawson, then the editor of *event,* for her encouragement. She not only printed the original article but made requests for others as well. She encouraged me further to make contact with Broadman about the possibility of collecting the series into a book.

Pat Tonroy and Merle Kirkby, secretaries of the Calvary Baptist Church in Garland, Texas, typed some of the early articles. Lavon Church and Phyllis Davis of the Southern Hills Baptist Church in Tulsa, where I now serve, typed the most recent articles.

A number of new chapters have been added to the pieces printed as articles. When they have all been put together in the final book form, I have Mildred Good to thank. She's a busy housewife, mother, and our church organist, but still took time to make sense of my rough drafts.

Charlie Shedd has proven an inspiration of longstanding. I attended a Christian Writers' Seminar with him some time ago. He encouraged my use of dialogue. I worked hard on his suggestions. We've corresponded about some of my style. He's made invaluable criticisms on the chapter entitled "When you Pray, Say . . ."

I see the book as being used in several different ways. I hope you read it and enjoy it. I hope it's a spiritual blessing to you.

Questions have been added to each chapter. View them

as spiritual probes. Some new flashes of insight might come as you think through them. The questions could be used along with the dialogues for retreat programs, Sunday School class meetings, fellowships, or any other thing that may come to mind.

Betty Jo, my wife, has always been my chief encourager. Whether I'm writing, preaching, pastoring a people . . . in good times and sad, whether high or low . . . she's made the positive difference.

So here you have it . . . *If God Talked Out Loud* . . . I'm praying for it to bless your life. God used its writing to teach and bless my own heart.

Yours for better praying,
CLYDE LEE HERRING

Contents

1.
When You Pray, Say . . .

Pray-er: "Our Father which art in heaven . . ."

GOD: *Yes?*

Pray-er: Don't interrupt me. I'm praying.

GOD: *But you called me.*

Pray-er: Called you? I didn't call you. I'm praying, "Our Father which art in heaven . . ."

GOD: *There, you did it again.*

Pray-er: Did what?

GOD: *Called me. You said, "Our Father which art in heaven." Here I am. What's on your mind?*

Pray-er: But I didn't mean anything by it. I was, you know, just saying my prayers for the day. I always say the Lord's Prayer. It makes me feel good, kind of like getting a duty done.

GOD: *All right. Go on.*

Pray-er: "Hallowed be thy name . . ."

GOD: *Hold it. What do you mean by that?*

Pray-er: By what?

GOD: *By "Hallowed be thy name"?*

Pray-er: It means . . . it means . . . good grief. I don't know what it means. How should I know? It's just part of the prayer. By the way, what does it mean?

GOD: *It means honored, holy, wonderful.*

Pray-er: Hey, that makes sense. I never thought what "hallowed" meant before. "Thy kingdom come. Thy will be done, in earth as it is in heaven."

GOD: *Do you really mean that?*

Pray-er: Sure, why not?

GOD: *What are you doing about it?*

Pray-er: Doing? Nothing, I guess. I just think it would be kind of neat if you got control of everything down here like you have up there.

GOD: *Have I got control of you?*

Pray-er: Well, I go to church.

GOD: *That isn't what I asked you. What about that habit of lust you have? And your bad temper? You've really got a problem there, you know. And then there's the way you spend your money . . . all on yourself. And what about the kind of books you read?*

Pray-er: Stop picking on me! I'm just as good as some of the rest of those phonies down at the church!

GOD: *Excuse me. I thought you were praying for my will to be done. If that is to happen, it will have to start with the ones who are praying it. Like you, for example.*

Pray-er: Oh, all right. I guess I do have some hang-ups. Now that you mention it, I could probably name some others.

GOD: *So could I.*

Pray-er: I haven't thought about it very much until now, but I really would like to cut out some of those things. I would like to, you know, be really free.

GOD: *Good! Now we're getting somewhere. We'll work together, you and I. Some victories can truly be won. I'm proud of you.*

Pray-er: Look, Lord, I need to finish up here. This is taking a lot longer than it usually does. "Give us this day our daily bread."

GOD: *You need to cut out the bread. You're overweight as it is.*

Pray-er: Hey, wait a minute! What is this, "Criticize Me Day"? Here I am, doing my religious duty, and all of a sudden you break in and remind me of all my hang-ups.

GOD: *Praying is a dangerous thing. You could wind up changed, you know. That's what I'm trying to get across to you. You called me, and here I am. It's too late to stop now. Keep on praying. I'm interested in the next part of your prayer . . . (Pause.) Well, go on.*

Pray-er: I'm scared to.

GOD: *Scared? Of what?*

Pray-er: I know what you'll say.

GOD: *Try me and see.*

Pray-er: "And forgive us our debts, as we forgive our debtors."

GOD: *What about Bill?* Susan

Pray-er: See? I knew it! I knew you would bring him up!
           Why, Lord, he's told lies about me, cheated me
           out of some money. He never paid back that debt
           he owes me. I've sworn to get even with him!

   GOD: *But your prayer? What about your prayer?*

Pray-er: I didn't mean it.

   GOD: *Well, at least you're honest. But it's not much fun
           carrying that load of bitterness around inside, is
           it?*

Pray-er: No. But I'll feel better soon as I get even. Boy,
           I've got some plans for old Bill! He'll wish he
           never did me any harm.

   GOD: *You won't feel any better. You'll feel worse. Re-
           venge isn't sweet. Think of how unhappy you al-
           ready are. But I can change all that.*

Pray-er: You can? How?

   GOD: *Forgive Bill. Then I'll forgive you. Then the hate
           and sin will be Bill's problem and not yours. You
           may lose the money, but you will have settled your
           heart.*

Pray-er: But Lord, I can't forgive Bill.

   GOD: *Then I can't forgive you.*

Pray-er: Oh, you're right. You always are. And more than I want revenge on Bill, I want to be right with you. *(Pause and sigh.)* All right. All right. I forgive him. Help him to find the right road in life, Lord. He's bound to be awfully miserable now that I think about it. Anybody who goes around doing the things she does to others has to be out of it. Someway, somehow, show him the right way.

GOD: *There, now! Wonderful! How do you feel?*

Pray-er: Hmmm. Well, not bad. Not bad at all. In fact, I feel pretty great! You know, I don't think I'll have to go to bed uptight tonight for the first time since I can remember. Maybe I won't be so tired from now on because I'm not getting enough rest.

GOD: *You're not through with your prayer. Go on.*

Pray-er: All right. "And lead us not into temptation, but deliver us from evil."

GOD: *Good! Good! I'll do that. Just don't put yourself in a place where you can be tempted.*

Pray-er: What do you mean by that?

GOD: *Quit hanging around the magazine stands where dirty books are sold. Change some of your friendships. Some of your so-called friends are beginning to get to you. They'll have you completely involved*

*in wrong things before long. Don't be foolish. They
advertise they're having fun, but for you it would
be ruin. Don't use me for an escape hatch.*

Pray-er: I don't understand.

GOD: *Sure you do. You've done it a lot of times. You
get caught in a bad situation. You get into trouble
and then you come running to me. "Lord, help me
out of this mess, and I promise you I'll never do
it again." You remember some of those bargains
you tried to make with me?*

Pray-er: Yes, and I'm ashamed, Lord. I really am.

GOD: *Which bargain are you remembering?*

Pray-er: Well, when the woman next door saw me backing
away from the neighborhood bar. I'd told mother
I was going to the store. I remember telling you,
"Oh, God, don't let her tell my mother where
I've been. I promise I'll be in church every Sun-
day."

GOD: *She didn't tell your mother, but you didn't keep
your promise, did you?*

Pray-er: I'm sorry, Lord. I really am. Up until now I
thought if I just prayed the Lord's Prayer every
day, then I could do what I liked. I didn't expect
anything to happen like it did.

GOD: *Go ahead and finish your prayer.*

Pray-er: "For thine is the kingdom, and the power, and the glory, for ever. Amen."

GOD: *Do you know what would bring me glory? What would really make me happy?*

Pray-er: No, but I'd like to know. Now I want to please you. I can see what a mess I've made of my life. And I can see how cool it would be to really be one of your followers.

GOD: *You just answered the question.*

Pray-er: I did?

GOD: *Yes. The thing that would bring me glory is to have people like you truly love me. And I see that happening between us. Now that some of these old sins are exposed and out of the way, well, there's no telling what we can do together.*

Pray-er: Lord, let's see what we can make of me, OK?

GOD: *Yes, let's see.*

Questions

1. Examine your prayer life. Do you tend to say the same things over and over again?

2. People may not repeat the Lord's Prayer, but may say things like: "Forgive me of all my sins." "Lead, guide, and direct me." "Bless all my family." The requests are good, but are often prayed without real meaning.

3. If God talked out loud to you while you prayed, what would he say? Try writing a prayer conversation between yourself and God. Think what God might reply. You may gain real spiritual insight as you follow through with the exercise.

4. Are there things you avoid praying about? What are they? Would prayer help change some actions you've been unable to change on your own?

Adapted from *event,* November 1973, pages 39-43. The Bible verses quoted are taken from the King James Version.

2.
Lord, Please Show Me Your Will

Sandy: O Lord, please show me your will for my life!

GOD: *All right.*

Sandy: What?

GOD: *I said, "All right."*

Sandy: But . . . I thought it would be harder than that. People are always saying how really hard it is to know and do what you want.

GOD: *Is that so?*

Sandy: Well, Lord, I heard this fellow give a testimony to our youth group. He talked about how he fought and fought against your will. He did exactly the opposite of your call. Now that he was old (I guess he must've been at least twenty-five), he had decided to surrender to you.

GOD: *Surrender, did he?*

Sandy: Well, yes. That's what he said. Lord, do I detect a little sarcasm in your voice today?

GOD: *You might at that.*

Sandy: But why?

GOD: *The idea of surrender is good sometimes—if a person means "surrender" in the sense of giving up his selfishness concerning my will. But the idea of "surrender" as some kind of personal martyrdom . . . well, you can see that's not what doing my will is all about.*

Sandy: But Lord, doing your will is hard. It requires sacrifice. It requires commitment. It requires doing something really against what a person wants to do . . . you know, like being a missionary to Africa or something.

GOD: *Want to know something really hard?*

Sandy: I guess.

GOD: *How about witnessing to the toad keepers in the zoo at Borneo or witnessing to the Oriental Used Car Dealers' Convention in Singapore?*

Sandy: You're making fun of me, Lord.

GOD: *Only trying to make a point with you.*

Sandy: I'm a little slow. I really don't understand. Everything I've ever thought about your will is that it's hard to understand and hard to do. In fact, it's like doing what one speaker to our youth group said.

GOD: *I've got a feeling which one you're about to quote, but go ahead.*

Sandy: Well, this fellow said, "The best way to know what God wants you to do is this: Figure out what you really want. Then do the opposite. God always works contrary to our desires."

GOD: *That hurts me.*

Sandy: Hurts you?

GOD: *Certainly. All of this makes it sound as if I'm some bad-tempered giant in the sky delighting in making things hard and burdensome for my people. Don't you see what all of this foolishness is leading to?*

Sandy: I don't guess I do.

GOD: *Look, Sandy. Here's just about the only conclusion you can draw. If you don't follow my will, I'm going to make your life miserable. If, on the other hand, you do follow my will, it's going to be so hard you'll be miserable. In other words, you can't win. It would be better never to know my will.*

Sandy: I never thought of it that way before.

GOD: That's obvious.

Sandy: But how am I supposed to think?

GOD: What kind of a God do you think I am? Am I mean, cruel, harsh, loving, kind, forgiving . . . what?

Sandy: Your Word says, "God is love."

GOD: Now we're getting someplace. If I love you, would I do something that would hurt you?

Sandy: No. Of course not. *(Pause.)* Hey, I'm beginning to see!

GOD: You've been acting as though I could hardly wait for you to "surrender" so I could really make life hard for you. While you can't ever really be in my place, try hard for a minute to answer this question: If you were God and one of your people asked to be shown your will, what would you do? Think about it. Would you, as a loving God, put him in a situation he couldn't handle? What would you do?

Sandy: No. If I were God, I'd match the need with the gifts of the person. Then I'd help that person have a desire to do the job.

GOD: I'm ahead of you.

Sandy: What do you mean?

GOD: *Get your Bible. Turn to Philippians 2:13. Read what it says.*

Sandy: OK. Hmmm . . . here it is. "For God is at work within you, helping you want to obey him, and then helping you do what he wants."

GOD: *See?*

Sandy: Things are beginning to shape up in my head. What you're saying is that when we really want to do your will, you help us want to do it.

GOD: *Right. I work on your "want to," not just your "ought to." If I only told you what you ought to do, then you might have a hard time. The part of you that was fearful or self-centered would fight against it. In other words, your "want to" might not want to do my will. But I love you. I want you to be willing to follow me cheerfully.*

Sandy: Well, I've sure learned something today. I guess that settles that.

GOD: *Not quite.*

Sandy: You mean there's more?

GOD: *You still have your Bible. Find Matthew 11:29-30.*

Sandy: Matthew 11:29-30 . . . OK, yeah. I've got it. "Wear
         my yoke—for it fits perfectly—and let me teach you;
         for I am gentle and humble, and you shall find
         rest for your souls; for I give you only light bur-
         dens."

         Why, there it is. Right there in front of me. You
         don't expect us to do more than we can accomplish,
         and you help us through even the toughest task.

GOD: *Now you're beginning to see.*

Sandy: Wow. I sure am glad. I just knew you were going
         to send me off to Africa where it'd be so hot I'd
         burn up.

GOD: *Some people want to go Africa. They want to go
         because I help them see not only that there is a
         need, but also that they can do a wonderful ministry
         there. If I want you to go to Africa, I'll give you
         specific talents which complement the work that's
         right for you.*

Sandy: That sure is a relief, Lord.

GOD: *Good. I hope so. But you've got something else to
         ask me, don't you?*

Sandy: Well, yes. I don't know exactly how to ask it. You
         know enough about me to realize that I frequently
         justify what I want to do by calling it your will.

GOD: *Yes, you* have *started learning a few things. What was the last big thing you did like that?*

Sandy: I remember mostly the car thing.

GOD: And how did you work that one out?

Sandy: I wanted that car so bad I almost got physically sick. It wasn't a big fancy car—just a little sporty-looking job.

GOD: See? You're doing it again.

Sandy: What do you mean?

GOD: You're beginning to justify your selfishness by saying that your desire for the smaller car was not nearly as selfish as a desire for a larger car would have been.

Sandy: I haven't learned all I should, I know. Anyway, that neat little red car just sat there at the car lot for several weeks. Every time I passed it I would say, "Lord, I sure would like that car. Nevertheless, not my will but thine be done."

GOD: That sounded very holy.

Sandy: It did to me.

GOD: What did you do next?

Sandy: One day I drove by and thought to myself, "Why,

it just might be God's will for me to have that car. With that car I could impress on people that you don't have to be an old 'stick-in-the-mud' to be a Christian. That little red car could probably make me a better witness. Yes, sir, I'm sure of it now. It's God's will for me to have that car." So I just turned around, went in, and bought it.

GOD: *You spent everything you'd saved, didn't you? Then you had to borrow some money for the insurance. Later you could see college coming up, and you had sunk all your money into something that would soon lose its value.*

Sandy: You knew about the transmission?

GOD: *I'm a transmission expert, Sandy.*

Sandy: Oh . . . yeah. I remember now. You know about everything. *(Pause.)* I admit it now, Lord. I can see what I did and how I did it. It was a terrible mistake, and it cost me a lot more than just money. That's what my question is all about. How can I tell whether an idea is just a justification of what I already want or truly your will?

GOD: *Ask yourself some questions, questions like: Is this going to bless others? Is it going to please God? If I do this, what will it do for my own spiritual life? Do I want to do it, or do I have a feeling that if I don't, I'll feel guilty?*

Sandy: I am learning. Really. I'm beginning to see what it's all about. Just because I want to do something doesn't make it automatically good or bad. It's the outcome that counts.

GOD: *Be in tune with the other voice in your head.*

Sandy: What do you mean?

GOD: *When you pray, I listen to what you say. I also listen to the other side of you. That side struggles against your spiritual side. It's that part of you that the devil works on and tries to make strong. That part doesn't want to do my will.*

Sandy: You know, Lord, I do remember thinking sometimes when I pray, "I don't really want to do this."

GOD: *That's what I mean. Be in tune with the part of your nature that welcomes my love for you. The devil will lie to you and say that my will is too hard, that there's not any fun in it, that you'll be miserable. If you really listen to that side, you will never do my will.*

Sandy: OK. Now I think I've got it. So show me your will for my life. What am I supposed to do for a career?

GOD: *What about tomorrow?*

Sandy: What about it?

 GOD: *What are you going to do about my will tomorrow?*

Sandy: Oh.

 GOD: *Yes . . . "Oh."*

Sandy: I didn't think about tomorrow. I just felt that I
       had to decide what I'm going to do with the rest
       of my life.

 GOD: *Turn to Luke 9:23-24. Read that passage.*

Sandy: Hmmm . . . OK. Got it. "Then he said to all,
       'Anyone who wants to follow me must put aside
       his own desires and conveniences and carry his
       cross with him every day and keep close to me!
       Whoever loses his life for my sake will save it,
       but whoever insists on keeping his life will lose
       it.' "

 GOD: *You see, it's the daily part that concerns me. Do
       my will every day, and step by step I'll reveal my
       overall plan for your life. Then each day will be
       just like another natural step for you . . . sometimes
       difficult or trying, but always wonderful and fulfill-
       ing.*

Sandy: Hey, I'm beginning to get really excited! Now I
       think I can figure out for the most part what you
       want me to do day by day. You've helped me with

that before. You mean if I do your will every day, then the overall plan for my life will come in time?

GOD: *That's right.*

Sandy: Lord, I feel so much better. Thank you. I won't have to go around frustrated because I don't know what you want me to do. In fact, now I'm excited about getting out there and doing your will today.

GOD: *I knew all along that you'd catch on, Sandy. When you're happy and enthusiastic about my will, that's the time to really get with it. And remember this: I'm always with you.*

Sandy: I'm really depending on you, Lord.

Questions

1. Discovering God's will for your life: (A) is hard to find out; (B) comes through a sudden revelation; (C) may happen over a period of time. Which of those answers would fit your view? Why?

2. After discovering God's will, do you believe it would be: (A) something you would really enjoy doing; (B) something you would really not like doing; (C) something that would make you lose your popularity with others? Which of those answers most closely fits your feelings about God's will? Why?

3. How can you tell the difference between God's will and human desire? What are some ways that can work for you?

4. What are some things you can be doing now while you wait until you know God's ultimate will for your future career?

Adapted from *event*, March 1976, pages 3-7. The Bible verses quoted are taken from *The Living Bible, Paraphrased* (Wheaton: Tyndale House Publishers, 1971), and are used by permission.

3.
Lord, I Don't Feel You When I Pray

Bob: Lord, I've got a problem. I don't feel you when I pray. At least sometimes I don't. I pray and pray, and nothing ever happens.

I don't feel anything.

Sometimes I pray about my problems, and the more I pray about them the more upset I become.

You know what I mean.

One of the problems I've been praying about is Randy. I don't know what I did to deserve him for a little brother. I know this: I wouldn't have chosen him if it had been up to me.

He's always making fun of me. If I get mad and start to hit him, he calls for Dad. "Bob, you cut that out!" Dad'll yell. "Don't pick on your little brother."

Randy just grins.

Like the other night. I was going on a date with Linda. She's very special to me. Dad loaned me the family car. I got really dressed up. I don't like to dress up—jeans are my thing—but I wanted to look good for Linda. I even used some of Dad's cologne. I thought I looked and smelled neat.

When I walked through the house, Randy laughed and said, "Whoooeee! Look at Bobby. Sniff, sniff. Smell him, too. He smells like a pig in a perfume parlor."

Lord, I think I could've killed him right then. I wanted to. I really did. "A pig in a perfume parlor."

I couldn't get it out of my mind. All the time I was with Linda I kept thinking, "Does she think I smell like a pig in a perfume parlor?"

I kept trying to smell myself. Once Linda asked, "Why do you keep sniffing all the time?"

I did it again. I said it all wrong. "I keep trying to smell the pig in a perfume parlor."

"Well, thanks a lot!" she said.

"No. No. I don't mean you. You don't stink like a pig. Why, you hardly smell bad at all."

She just stared at me. Big tears came down her cheeks. Very softly she said, "Take me home."

I knew I couldn't talk my way out of it. I'd probably have made it worse.

On my way back home, I got so mad at Randy I couldn't think. He did it! He said, "Pig in a perfume parlor." If he hadn't said it, everything would've been all right.

I'm going to give him a shot in the mouth when I get home. I don't care what Dad says. I may even kill him.

No. No. I can't do that. It would only make it worse. I can't kill him. I can't even give him a knuckle sandwich. There's only one thing to do—pray. So I prayed. Like I'm doing now. I didn't feel anything. No. That's not right. I felt something. I felt mad.

I'm getting mad again like the other night. The more I pray, the madder I get.

When I talk to you, my prayers don't get beyond the ceiling.

GOD: *They don't have to get beyond the ceiling.*

Bob: What?

GOD: *I'm not in the attic.*

Bob: Is that you, Lord?

GOD: *Who have you been talking to?*

Bob: You.

GOD: *Does it surprise you that I'd be here?*

Bob: I guess so, yes. After all, I've been praying and

praying, and I haven't felt anything at all.

GOD: *Maybe it's because you do all the talking.*

Bob: What?

GOD: *Remember the advice I gave to people in my Word?*

Bob: You gave a lot of advice.

GOD: *The one about being still.*

Bob: Oh . . . the place where you say, "Be still and know that I am God"?

GOD: *That's the one. You're so busy going over your problems when you pray that you don't think about me.*

Bob: What else am I supposed to do? Prayer is talking— so I talk about my problems. When I do, I get mad all over again.

GOD: *You're partly right.*

Bob: What do you mean?

GOD: *Prayer is talking about your problems. But there's something more. Prayer is meditating. Being calm. Opening up your heart and mind. Remember, I'm not way off. I'm here with you.*

Bob: Sometimes I forget.

GOD: *Even when you forget, I'm still with you.*

Bob: But what if I don't feel anything?

GOD: *Feelings come and go. I am with you always.*

Bob: I think you said that in the Bible.

GOD: *Good for you. You're remembering some Scripture.*

Bob: But I want to *feel* something when I pray. I want to feel happy, or peaceful, or *something*.

GOD: *You will.*

Bob: You've confused me again.

GOD: *You'll have good feelings in time if you really believe I'm always with you. Sometimes other feelings or a wandering mind may block your awareness of me. Keep remembering that my presence doesn't depend on your feelings. As your anger quietens, you'll begin to realize I'm in your heart.*

Bob: I'm feeling better right now, Lord.

GOD: *Listening to me will do you good.*

Bob: I'd like to feel good all the time.

GOD: *I never promised my followers they would always feel good. If you read about my conversations with Peter and the others, you'll discover I didn't feel good all the time.*

Bob: You didn't?

GOD: *Do you remember the boat trip on the Sea of Galilee?*

Bob: The one when the storm came?

GOD: *Yes. What happened?*

Bob: Well, the storm came. The boat was about to sink. All the disciples were afraid.

GOD: *And where was I?*

Bob: Let's see. Oh, I remember. You were in the back of the boat, asleep. I think the Bible says you were tired.

GOD: *Do you feel good when you're tired?*

Bob: No. I guess you didn't either.

GOD: *Do you remember the donkey incident?*

Bob: The donkey incident?

GOD: *The white one.*

Bob: Oh . . . the triumphant entry.

GOD: That's the one.

Bob: That must've been great. All of those people lining the streets, laying palm branches and cloaks on the road. Yes, that must've made you feel great. I'd like to feel that way.

GOD: I don't think you read all the story. Find Luke 19:28-44.

Bob: OK. I've got the story. Hmmmm . . . It says you looked over the city of Jerusalem and cried.

GOD: How do you feel when you cry?

Bob: I'm sad. I'm beginning to see that you didn't always feel great.

GOD: I'm always with you, whether or not you feel good. My presence doesn't depend on your feelings. I was with you when you were embarrassed. I was there when you were angry with Randy.

Bob: I don't think I'll ever be the same again, Lord. I doubted your presence because I couldn't feel you. Now I see you'll always be with me, no matter how I feel or what happens.

GOD: Wonderful. You learn . . . often the hard way, but you learn.

Bob: I know I've learned a lot today.

GOD: *Bob, there's something else.*

Bob: Yes, Lord, what is it?

GOD: *You don't smell like a pig in a perfume parlor.*

Bob: Thanks, Lord. I needed that.

Questions

1. Almost everyone feels that he fails to get through to God at times. When you don't feel the spiritual closeness to God, what is your reaction? Do you get discouraged? Try harder? Talk to someone?

2. If someone told you about his problem with prayer, what would you advise him to do?

3. Bob discovered one of the secrets to feeling good. As you think about it, put it in your own words.

4. How could you change your own prayer life to be even more open to God's presence?

4.
I Need Some Luck, Lord, and Hurry!

Sandy: I need some luck, Lord. And hurry. *(Pause.)* Lord? Are you there?

GOD: *I'm here.*

Sandy: Did you hear me?

GOD: *I heard.*

Sandy: Well . . . I'm waiting. Send me some luck.

GOD: *I don't deal in "luck."*

Sandy: Wait a minute. What do you mean . . . you don't deal in luck?

GOD: *I think the statement is clear.*

Sandy: Oh, man, I'm in trouble.

GOD: *What have you done?*

Sandy· It's not what I've done. It's what I haven't done.

GOD: *What did you leave undone?*

Sandy: I've got a big test coming up in history this morning. I put off studying until late last night. I get confused. All those dates and people . . . the Seven Years' War . . . the Hapsburgs . . . the French Revolution. I don't know the difference between "Holy Cow" and the Holy Roman Empire.

GOD: *There is a difference.*

Sandy: That's why I need you. You were there. I wasn't. You should be able to tell me all about it. Why, having you with me when I take the test will be like having an eyewitness to answer all the questions.

GOD: *I agree.*

Sandy: With what?

GOD: *You're in trouble.*

Sandy: You mean you won't help me?

GOD: *I didn't say that. I'll help you remember what you've applied yourself to learn.*

Sandy: What good is prayer if I'm going to have to do

it all myself? If there's no advantage to praying, then you should've told me a long time ago.

GOD: *There's every advantage to praying. You gain an awareness of me. You experience peace in your heart. You receive power to perform at your very best.*

Sandy: But you said in your Word, "Ask, and ye shall receive. Knock, and it shall be opened unto you."

GOD: *I keep my promises.*

Sandy: Good. Now we've got it straight. I'm asking. Send me some good luck for the test tomorrow.

GOD: *Sorry.*

Sandy: Now look, Lord. I asked. You said I'd receive. So here I am.

GOD: *You didn't ask right.*

Sandy: What am I supposed to do, say, "Pretty please with a cherry on top"?

GOD: *I don't need cherries.*

Sandy: Well, I need some luck, Lord.

GOD: *If you had asked, "Help me to do my best," your request would have been answered.*

Sandy: I need a lot more than my best. I'll flunk that test for sure if all I do is my best. I haven't studied enough. I know that.

Well, if you don't send me some luck, I'll have to do something else.

GOD: What are you getting out of your sock drawer?

Sandy: You can be sure it's not socks.

GOD: What have you got in your hand?

Sandy: It's my good-luck peach pit.

GOD: Your good-luck peach pit?

Sandy: Sure. I found it last summer at church camp. It was lying on the ground near where we had the services each evening. I broke it in half. It has this little round indention in the center, just right to rub with my thumb. I stuck it in my pocket and started rubbing it. See how shiny it is?

GOD: I see.

Sandy: The way I had it figured is that you blessed the camp. Many people were touched by you, and lots of lives were changed. I thought, "God must've blessed this little seed, too. I'll carry it around with me. It will bring me blessings and good luck."

GOD: Does it work?

Sandy: Does it ever. Whenever I take out this peach pit and rub it, good things happen. It always works.

GOD: *Always?*

Sandy: Sure.

GOD: *Always?*

Sandy: Well, not quite. But usually, really. Not long after I found it, our football team was playing one of our chief rivals. We were behind in the fourth quarter. I got out my good-luck piece and rubbed and prayed. We had a tremendous fourth quarter and won the game.

GOD: *The peach pit did it, you think.*

Sandy: I think so, yes. Up until the fourth quarter, we weren't doing very good. After I started rubbing on the ol' peach pit, things changed.

GOD: *The team didn't have anything to do with it?*

Sandy: A little, maybe.

GOD: *Did your good-luck piece make the last touchdown?*

Sandy: No.

GOD: *Did it make the saving tackle in the last minute of the game?*

Sandy: No, I guess not. It sounds like you know about the game.

GOD: *A little, yes. For your information, the peach pit didn't have anything to do with it.*

Sandy: I don't know about that. All I know is that when I rubbed it we did better—when I didn't we didn't do well. It was kind of like Moses. When his arms were held up high, his army defeated the enemy. When he got tired and his arms fell, the enemy won. Then his men came and held his arms high so that the forces of God could win.

GOD: *You and Moses now, is it?*

Sandy: Right. He had his rod you had blessed. I have my peach pit.

GOD: *The rod of God and the blessed peach pit.*

Sandy: That's the way I see it. I believe you've blessed this seed of a peach just like you blessed Moses' rod. Whenever I rub it, you will give me what I wish for.

(*Sandy vigorously rubs her peach pit.*)

There . . . that ought to do it. I'll do it one more time and wish really hard . . . . "I wish I could do well on the history test."

GOD: *Feel any smarter?*

Sandy: Not yet, but I will. I feel confident now. Even though prayer didn't help me, my good-luck piece will.

(Later in the day, Sandy returns to her room. The test is over. Depressed, she turns to the Lord in prayer.) Lord, are you there?

GOD: *I'm here. How was the test?*

Sandy: Rugged.

GOD: *Did the peach pit help?*

Sandy: Frankly, no.

GOD: *Tell me about it.*

Sandy: I can hear Mrs. Simmons now. "All right, class. Get out your pens. This is the major test in history. Half of your entire grade will depend on how well you do." I felt my stomach get tight. My head throbbed.

Then I remembered the lucky peach seed in my pocket. I put my hand in and touched it. It was a real comfort. I got it out and looked at it. I was admiring it when Mrs. Simmons came down the aisle, passing out the tests. "What are you doing, Sandy?" she asked.

I said, "Uh—just looking at this old peach seed." "I see," she said. She looked at me kind of funny. She raised her right eyebrow like she does when she thinks a kid is kind of dumb.

"Well, plant your seed in your desk. This is test time." She thought it was cute. Some of the other kids giggled. It didn't matter. That peach seed was blessed by you. It was going to bring me good luck.

GOD: *You look depressed. Go on with your story.*

Sandy: I rubbed that peach seed and said something like, "OK. This is it. Bring me luck." Then I put it in my pocket. I felt good. I had confidence that I was going to really come through on the test.

GOD: *Even though you hadn't studied?*

Sandy: Right. That's what I thought until . . .

GOD: *Until?*

Sandy: Until . . . until . . . well, until I saw the very first question. "Modern-day Istanbul has gone by what other names in her history?" The second question was, "What were the dates given on which the names of the city were changed?" I thought to myself, "Other names of Istanbul? What other names? Good grief. I don't even know where Istanbul is. Maybe some of these other questions are easier."

I looked. They weren't. "Napoleon Bonaparte was exiled to what island in what year?"

What popped in my mind was Napoleon's picture. He always has a hand stuffed inside the buttons of his vest. I thought about writing, "I'll tell you what island he went to if you'll tell me why Napoleon had to scratch his chest so much."

GOD: *You didn't know the answers.*

Sandy: No. I kept thinking, "Any minute now the answers will start flowing. That ol' peach pit is really going to give me the luck I need."

GOD: *And?*

Sandy: And nothing. I struggled as best I could, but nothing happened.

GOD: *What did you do with the peach seed?*

Sandy: I took it out of my pocket on the way home. I said, "Seed, you're nothing but a lousy failure. You didn't bring me any luck. First prayer, and now this." Then I threw it away.

GOD: *What kind of conclusion did you reach?*

Sandy: I didn't do well on the test. If I passed the course, I'll be lucky . . .

GOD: *Lucky?*

Sandy: Well, . . . you know what I mean. I'll be fortunate.

GOD: *Neither. You'll get what you deserved. If you learned enough to pass, it will show. If not, it's not because of bad luck or that prayer failed. It will be because you didn't apply yourself.*

Sandy: I guess that's part of my conclusion. I thought prayer and good luck were part of the same thing. I figured prayer was kind of like a lucky charm. You would come in and rescue me, even if I didn't do my part.

GOD: *What have you learned about prayer?*

Sandy: I've learned that prayer really works to help me be in control, do my best, and have a sense of your presence. I know now you'll help me do my best, but prayer isn't magic.

GOD: *Good. Good. You've passed the test.*

Sandy: I did? I passed the history test?

GOD: *No. The prayer test.*

Sandy: Oh. Well . . . shoot, that's even better. I learned something today about prayer I'll never forget.

GOD: *You're way ahead. Some people never learn about prayer and keep thinking it will bring them the kind of luck they need. All their lives they never apply themselves. They simply wait for me to do what they could have done if they used what I had already given them.*

Sandy: I may have passed. I may have failed. I don't know. I do know this; next time, I'm going to study my head off. When I go to the next test, I'll ask you to help me do my best.

 GOD: Now you're getting smart.

Sandy: Thank you, Lord. I've been dumb long enough. It's time I get smart about some things.

Questions

1. What is *luck* to you? How many people believe in luck? Do you have any good-luck pieces? Why do you think your good-luck piece works?

2. In what ways do you think people connect luck and prayer? What is the difference between luck and prayer?

3. How does prayer help in day-by-day circumstances?

4. How should a person pray when he comes to test times or other difficult situations?

5.
Lord, I Get Scared When I Think About Dying

Bob: Lord, I'm really scared.

GOD: *About what?*

Bob: I feel guilty, too.

GOD: *Those are bad feelings. What's troubling you?*

Bob: I get scared when I think about dying. Then I feel guilty. Christians aren't supposed to be afraid of dying.

GOD: *Tell me about your feelings. What started this?*

Bob: I'm really a happy-go-lucky sort of a guy. I like to have fun. I'm not the serious type, you know.

GOD: *I've noticed.*

Bob: Oh yes, I suppose you have. Anyway, I haven't ever had anyone close to me die. Susan called a couple of days ago. She told me Larry had just been killed. He was riding his motorcycle when a drunk driver veered right at him. Larry turned his motorcycle off the road as quick as he could. His cycle flipped over. He was thrown a long way off and hit his head. Susan told me he died almost instantly.

I was so stunned I could hardly say anything. Larry had given me a ride on his motorcycle earlier in the day. He was a happy guy like me. He didn't cause anybody any problems. He just wanted to have a good time and do a lot of things in life.

Yesterday a lot of his friends gathered at the funeral home. Just being there scared me.

GOD: *You must have been very troubled. Keep on with your story. It will help sort out all the fears and confusion you feel.*

Bob: Lord, I don't know how it happened. I've never been to a funeral before. I'd never even been in a funeral home. I'd never seen any dead bodies. Not really. I know the difference between someone really dying and all those people that get killed on TV.

Several of us went into the room where Larry's body was. He was lying there in the casket. He was dressed in a suit with a shirt and tie on. I hardly ever remember seeing him dressed like that. He looked like he was asleep, but we all knew it was permanent.

GOD: *What was going on inside you?*

Bob: I wanted to cry. I wanted to run. I wanted to yell at him to get up so we could get out of the place. I even felt sick at my stomach.

GOD: *You didn't do any of that, did you?*

Bob: No. It seemed as though everyone acted the same way. Organ music came over the intercom system. The smell of fresh carnations filled the room.

GOD: *How did people act?*

Bob: Most of them spoke quietly. People looked serious. Some even cried, especially when Larry's parents came in. It nearly got to me when I saw Larry's little brother, Mark.

Mark tried to do everything Larry did. When Mark broke down and cried, I had to leave. It was too much for me.

I walked to the door of the funeral home. As soon as I could see no one was watching, I ran as fast as I could to the car. When I finally got away, I stopped in a nearby park. I laid my head over on the steering wheel and cried like a baby.

GOD: *What about later? During the night?*

Bob: That's when it really began to get bad, Lord. I thought, *If Larry could die, so could I. I don't want to die. I don't even want to think about dying.* The more I thought about not wanting to die, the more it seemed to haunt me. I couldn't get away from the picture in the funeral home, seeing Larry lying there so still.

It wasn't long before I began to feel like I could die any minute. The more I thought about it, the more certain I became. I was afraid to go to sleep. I thought I would probably never wake up.

Oh, Lord, just talking to you about it gets me upset again. Why did Larry have to die? Why does anyone have to die? Why do I have to die someday?

GOD: *Now we're at the heart of the matter. Those are questions from deep inside you. You really do need them answered. I can help.*

Bob: Oh, I was sure hoping so. If you couldn't help me get over this, I think it would be easier to go crazy or something . . .

GOD: *There's one more question you haven't asked out loud. What is it?*

Bob: I feel guilty even thinking it. Still, Lord, I've heard so much about it the last two days that it's really burning inside.

GOD: *Go on.*

Bob: Larry had a lot of Christian friends. Many of them

kept telling his family and his other friends, "It was the will of God for Larry to die. You've got to accept it."

GOD: Do you believe them?

Bob: They all acted so certain. Maybe they were right. Maybe it was your will for Larry to die. But why? What had he done? How come you took it out on him? There are people a lot worse than he ever was, and they seem to be doing just fine.

GOD: Follow your thinking for a moment.

Bob: I don't understand.

GOD: If it was my will for Larry to die, what does that make me?

Bob: Well, if another human being were to do something like that, we would call him a killer or something. I can't call you a killer.

GOD: What did I say about killing?

Bob: I remember that one of the Ten Commandments was about it. You said, "Thou shalt not kill."

GOD: I can tell you not to kill while I am busy killing people all the time. Does that seem like clear thinking to you?

Bob: If you did things like that, you would be contradicting yourself. You can't do that.

GOD: *Think hard for a moment. Tell me of someone I harmed when I walked the earth.*

Bob: I wish I knew the Bible better. Let me see . . . hmmmm. No, I can't think of anytime you harmed someone.

GOD: *Can you remember anyone who was helped?*

Bob: Oh, many. Blind people were made to see; sick people were made well; even some dead people came alive. As I remember it, you were kind of a walking hospital ward because so many sick people followed.

GOD: *What is your conclusion?*

Bob: You didn't kill Larry. But wait a minute. If you didn't kill Larry, how come he's dead?

GOD: *Who caused the accident?*

Bob: The fellow who had been drinking too much. He simply didn't know what he was doing. He drove right at Larry. Larry had to go off the road! His motorcycle flipped.

GOD: *Did I make the man drink?*

Bob: No, of course not. He did it on his own.

GOD: *Did I make him drive?*

Bob: No. He drove on his own. The newspaper article about it said the bartender told him he ought to get someone to help him get home safely.

GOD: *You see, Bob, if I am responsible for Larry's death, I'm also responsible for the man's drunkenness. What would you think of some man who did things like that?*

Bob: We'd lock him up quick before he did any more harm.

GOD: *Do you believe I am worse than criminals?*

Bob: No. I'm beginning to see, I think. Larry's death was caused by someone else. The man who did it was responsible. Not you. Your Word says, "God is love." A loving God doesn't go around killing people.

GOD: *I'm glad to be found innocent.*

Bob: But Lord, why do people always say that such tragic things are your will?

GOD: *People want to say something helpful. They believe they can help the sorrowing by making the statement, "It's God's will."*

Bob: But why?

GOD: *People who have lost loved ones ask many questions. Some questions seem to have no answers. Often they get bitter and depressed.*

Bob: What has that got to do with the statement about your will?

GOD: *If people believe every tragedy is my will, then the questions aren't asked. They accept the fate that has come their way.*

Bob: That's terrible.

That's terrible.

If they ever stopped to think what all of it means, it would cause more problems than it solves.

GOD: *Not everyone accepts the statement. Some believe me to be loving as my Word says. Others believe that I am responsible and become angry.*

Bob: I admit I was angry. I'm not anymore. I know you didn't do it.

GOD: *I'll tell you something that is my will in Larry's death.*

Bob: What could it possibly be?

GOD: *Turn to John 14:1-3. What does it say?*

Bob: OK. John 14. All right. Here it is. "Let not your

heart be troubled. You are trusting God, now trust in me. There are many homes up there where my Father lives, and I am going to prepare them for your coming. When everything is ready, then I will come and get you, so that you can always be with me where I am. If this weren't so, I would tell you plainly."

GOD: *My will for Larry's future is clear enough, don't you think?*

 Bob: I know Larry was a Christian. Because he trusted you, you have a place for him in heaven. You even prepared it for him yourself.

Lord, I'm feeling better. Not just about Larry, but about myself.

GOD: *Good. Keep on thinking. Get it clear so you'll know what's making it work in your heart.*

 Bob: I'm feeling better because I know you didn't take Larry's life. I was having a terrible problem with the thought. Also, I'm not worried about Larry. No matter how people die, you have a better plan for their lives.

Reading the passage in John really helped me. It says a Christian doesn't have to be afraid of death. If we have you in our hearts, you will make it so we can be with you in heaven.

GOD: *There. I'm glad you're feeling better.*

Bob: But Lord . . .

GOD: Yes?

Bob: I still don't want to die.

GOD: Good. Live as long as you can. Work hard. Take care of yourself. There's plenty of time in heaven when you get here.

Bob: I'm glad to hear you say so. You know, I'm really happy I know you. Death doesn't seem so scary now, and Larry's obviously still alive with you. I really thank you for this time. I'll never forget it.

Questions

1. Some say that when a person dies, he's just like an animal . . . death ends his existence. Do you agree? What do you think happens when a person dies? Why do people become so afraid when they think about death?

2. What are some of the promises of the Bible about eternal life? What do you expect heaven to be like?

3. Do you believe God is responsible for every death? Are there ways in which human beings cause death without God's causing it? Is every tragedy the will of God?

4. Read John 14:1-3 and Revelation 21:3-4; 22:1-5. Do these passages change your views about heaven?

The Bible verse quoted is taken from *The Living Bible, Paraphrased* (Wheaton: Tyndale House Publishers, 1971), and is used by permission.

6.
You're a Winner

GOD: *You're depressed tonight.*

Bob: Dumb!

GOD: *And angry.*

Bob: Dumb!

GOD: *You're not going to speak to me?*

Bob: Dumb. Double dumb!

GOD: *My name is not "Dumb."*

Bob: Oh, I know, Lord. But . . but . . oh, I'm so dumb.

GOD: *What's wrong? Come on, tell me. If you don't you stand a chance of blowing up, as angry as you are.*

Bob: I did it again. You know how dumb I am. Just

about the time I think I have things pretty well under control, I say something stupid and put my foot in my mouth, and everybody laughs at me.

GOD: *What did you do this time?*

Bob: See? See? Even you. You do it. You said, "What did you do this time?" I even have a record of dumb stunts with you. You even expect me to do it.

GOD: *I was only agreeing with you. And, yes, you do have quite a record.*

Bob: See?

GOD: *So?*

Bob: What do you mean, "So"?

GOD: *I mean it doesn't affect my feelings for you, my faith in you.*

Bob: But, Lord, this time was worse than ever.

GOD: *Tell me.*

Bob: OK. Well, I was at the church banquet. I really felt that I was in good control. The whole thing was going really well, you know? I had on this new suit, had my hair styled, and man . . .

GOD: *Wait a minute.*

Bob: What?

GOD: *I'm God, not "man."*

Bob: Oh, I'm sorry. Sometimes I feel so close to you, I think of you as my friend instead of God.

GOD: *I'm both, and that's better. Because I'm God I can know you better than any friend and love you more than all your friends put together.*

Bob: Well, right now you're probably the *only* friend I've got. I blew it tonight. I really did. Dumb! Dumb! Dumb! Nobody will have anything to do with me anymore.

GOD: *Go on.*

Bob: Well, I had this real neat girl with me, you know? Do you know Jane Ellen Banks?

GOD: *Pretty well, yes.*

Bob: Ha! I forgot again. You know everybody. Anyway, she's really something. All the other guys were really envious of me. I mean, she's really got it.

GOD: *Watch your thoughts.*

Bob: Oh, yeah. Well, we went to the fellowship hall, and do you know what I did? I sat down without holding the chair for her. Dumb! She just stood there, waiting for me to realize what had happened. When I saw what I had done I jumped up out of my chair; then my knee hit the table top, and I turned over two glasses of water! Two! Oh, it was awful, really awful. Right in my lap, too.

GOD: *I know.*

Bob: It was terrible! I just stood there and looked at myself. I couldn't do a thing. I was so embarrassed, I wanted to die; but I couldn't. What was worse, it got worse. You know Mrs. Murdock, the big heavyset lady? She's the one who's always doing so much for people. She heard the noise I had made and came out of the kitchen. She hurried over to where I was standing, just frozen, looking at myself. Then she said, "Why, little Bob (I hate it when people call me that!), whatever did you do?" Well, that brought a roar from everyone. Even Jane Ellen laughed.

GOD: *Shh! Be calm. It's over now. I know it was rough.*

Bob: Besides, that wasn't all. I made another classic boo-boo later.

GOD: *Get it all off your chest.*

Bob: Somehow or another I got calmed down, and finally the food was served. By this time I was really starving. Looking back on it, I sure wish I had listened to my dad when he was trying to teach me some table manners. But no, the only thing I'm interested in when I sit down at the table is devouring anything that's edible. I can't blame my folks for what happened at the banquet. They tried to teach me.

GOD: *What happened?*

Bob: Well, the speaker had gotten up to talk before we had finished eating. And he was good. He was telling a bunch of jokes. Everybody was laughing. I'd just about forgotten what I had done earlier. Anyway, I had just put a big mouthful of mashed potatoes with gravy in my mouth and had taken another big bite of those cold, hard rolls they always serve at church banquets. And he did it! The guy told one of the funniest jokes I'd ever heard in all my life. I forgot what was in my mouth and just started laughing. Well, out it came! Crumbs from the roll spewed everywhere—on Jane Ellen's dress, on her plate, on the paper tablecloth—everywhere. When everyone saw what I had done, they laughed even harder at me than they did at the joke. Oh, but that's not all!

GOD: *I'm listening.*

Bob: Jane Ellen didn't live very far from the church, so I walked her home. Lord, you know I didn't mean anything by trying to kiss Jane Ellen. I thought if I did I'd forget what I'd done, and at least something good would've happened for the night. I'm not very experienced. We stood on her front porch. I said, "Good night." She said, "Good night." But she didn't go in, and I didn't leave. I stood on one foot and then on the other. She looked shy and embarrassed. Finally our eyes met and we both knew what we wanted to do. She shut her eyes, then opened them again and looked up at me. I shut my eyes and leaned in the direction where I thought she would be. God, this is so terrible!

GOD: *Try to finish!*

Bob: Well, I leaned toward her at the same time she was leaning toward me, and instead of our lips meeting, we bumped heads. *I mean hard!* That did it. She opened her eyes, and anger flashed. She turned around, opened the door, went in, and slammed it without even as much as another "Good night." If I live to be a thousand, I hope I never have another day like this one.

GOD: *You won't.*

Bob: What? Have another day like this one?

GOD: *No. Live to be a thousand.*

Bob: Well, thank goodness for that. I don't want to live another day if I'm going to keep doing dumb, stupid things like I did. Lord, you know it just looks like I'm a born loser. Sometimes I think I can never do anything right. Is my life just going to be one constant mess-up after another?

GOD: You're a winner.

Bob: You know I just keep doing them over and over again . . . What did you say?

GOD: I said, "You're a winner."

Bob: Don't kid me, Lord. Not you. I don't think I could take it from you, too.

GOD: I repeat, "You're a winner."

Bob: Could you explain that? I mean, after what I did tonight, how in the world could I be a winner?

GOD: You can't be.

Bob: Please, Lord. This double-talk boggles my brain. What do you mean?

GOD: You said, "How in the world could I be a winner?" You can't be a winner "in the world." The secret is to win outside the world. The secret is you and me working together. Think for a moment. What can make a loser into a winner?

Bob: Well, I guess . . . sure! I know! It's you. Even your Word says, "If God be for us, who can be against us?" And it also says, "We are more than conquerors through him that loved us."

GOD: *See, some of that Bible reading is paying off! You're exactly right. Now pick yourself up. Don't go around tomorrow as if you were a loser. That's an insult to me. Let the others laugh at you. Laugh at yourself a little. You'll have to admit you were the life of the banquet. Here, now, it's time for some rest. Don't worry about things. Tomorrow is another day. I'll never leave you. Remember, I'm in the business of making winners out of losers.*

Bob: I must be going to be the biggest winner you ever saw. I mean, if you can do anything with me, by contrast with the mess I made tonight, I'll really be something.

GOD: *You will be.*

Bob: What?

GOD: *Really something. Sleep well . . . winner.*

Questions

1. What does the word *winner* mean to you? What do you think it means to others?

2. Almost everyone has failed and had embarrassing moments. How do those times make you feel? Do you think of yourself as a loser?

3. How does God make winners out of losers? What are some of the advantages Christians have that others do not have in becoming winners in life?

4. What would you tell persons who thought of themselves as losers? How could you help them change their minds about themselves?

Adapted from *event*, October 1975, pages 27-31.

7.
All I Ever Hear is Rules, Rules, Rules!

Sandy: All I ever hear is rules, rules, rules! I get sick and tired of rules!

GOD: *You're upset again.*

Sandy: You're right, Lord. I've had it up to here. I can't take any more. Every time I want to do something, someone seems to think of some rule or reason why I can't do it.

GOD: *Give me some examples.*

Sandy: Examples . . . examples!? My whole life is one big example of what I'm talking about. "Don't do this. Don't do that. Stop doing whatever it is you're doing. No, you can't go there. No, you can't do that. Stop chewing your gum. Always be nice. Always be good."

GOD: *Be careful. You might explode.*

Sandy: Well, I might, but there's probably some rule

against it. "Thou shalt not explode thyself," or something like that.

GOD: *Tell me what started this outburst.*

Sandy: You've heard of the straw that broke the camel's back?

GOD: *Yes, I think I've heard it before.*

Sandy: Oh, I keep forgetting that you always know everything.

GOD: *Go on. Tell me what bothered you so much.*

Sandy: Yesterday we had this basketball game. It was really a good game. We were playing our arch rivals. We hadn't beaten them in a long time, but last night our guys really came through. We won the game. You wouldn't believe how happy we all were.

GOD: *I know you were happy.*

Sandy: Oh, yeah. You know about our feelings, too. Anyway, all the kids decided they would go out and celebrate winning the game . . .

GOD: *All the kids?*

Sandy: Sure. All the kids. Everybody was going out to this ice-cream place, and . . .

GOD: *All the kids? Everybody?*

Sandy: Well, maybe not everybody.

GOD: *That's more honest. You see, I overheard what you told your parents on the phone.*

Sandy: What'd I say? I forgot.

GOD: *You do forget every now and then when it's convenient. You said, "Dad, may I go to the ice-cream shop with all the other kids? Everybody is going."*

Sandy: What's wrong with that? If other kids can go, I don't know why I can't.

GOD: *Not all the other kids went, remember?*

Sandy: OK, Lord. Some of the kids. But I wanted to go so bad. Everyone was happy. We were going to have lots of fun. I can't understand why I couldn't go.

GOD: *What did your dad say?*

Sandy: I don't want to talk about it.

GOD: *I think you started this conversation.*

Sandy: It wasn't what he said. It's what he asked.

GOD: *And what was that?*

Sandy: He asked, "Did you do your homework?"

GOD: Had you done it?

Sandy: No, but you know how I am, Lord. I always put things off. Besides, I could've done it after I got back.

GOD: What was the rule?

Sandy: The rule was that I couldn't go out unless I had done all my homework.

GOD: Did you understand the rule and agree with it?

Sandy: Yes, but that was before we won the game. It was before all the other kids were going out together. It was before I wanted to go out so much.

GOD: Why was the rule set up?

Sandy: My dad said I needed to have more self-discipline. He said if I got into bad habits of putting things off, I would always find myself behind in my work when I got grown. It made sense to me at the time.

GOD: Now that you think about it, does it still make sense?

Sandy: I suppose so—it's just that everywhere I turn, there are rules that seem to keep me from having a good time.

GOD: *I'm sorry you feel sad, but rules really help make you a better person. I remember another rule you set up and then broke on your own.*

Sandy: Which one?

GOD: *You remember the skateboard incident?*

Sandy: Do I? How can I ever forget it? Little Howie next door was trying to learn to ride his skateboard. I watched him in his driveway. He kept falling off. I thought I'd go over and give him a few pointers. I was known as the "skateboard champ" of the neighborhood a couple of years back when they were popular then.

GOD: *What did you do?*

Sandy: I said, "Now, Howie, if you're going to ride this thing, there are a few rules you've got to always keep in mind. If you break any of these rules, you could get wiped out in more ways than one. Rule number 1 is this: never, ever ride your skateboard into the street without looking to see if anyone is coming."

GOD: *What happened then?*

Sandy: I showed him how to keep his balance, how to make those neat turns, how to get up good speed so he could coast a long way.

GOD: *Something else happened, didn't it?*

Sandy: How was I to know that guy would be riding a bicycle down the street just then?

GOD: *That was the reason for the rule, wasn't it?*

Sandy: I suppose so. Anyway, I really got up some speed. I was sort of showing off for Howie, showing him how good I was. I didn't even think about looking. I didn't hear any cars. If that guy on the bike had yelled, it wouldn't have been so bad.

GOD: *He did yell.*

Sandy: Not soon enough. I was sailing down the driveway, out into the street, when suddenly I heard this guy say, "Yeooww!" and BAM, I rammed him. He went one way; I fell over on his bike; and Howie's skateboard got all splintered up. Boy, did that ever hurt. But what was worse was what Howie said.

GOD: *And what was that?*

Sandy: He said, "Rule number 1 is never, never, ever ride your skateboard into the street without looking to see if anyone is coming. HAHAHAHA!"

GOD: *What did you say?*

Sandy: I said, "Now you see why? You could get creamed like I did. So remember the rule." I limped home and haven't been on a skateboard since. I was really embarrassed.

GOD: *Are you telling me that rules aren't all bad?*

Sandy: I guess I am, Lord, come to think about it. If I had kept that rule, I wouldn't have been so hurt or embarrassed. If I had finished my homework, my dad probably would've let me go out with the other kids. Good rules really help in the long run. Yes, Lord, rules are good for us. If we keep those good rules, our lives will be better and happier all the way around.

GOD: *Thank you for your sermon.*

Sandy: Uh . . . I guess you already knew those things about rules anyway.

GOD: *Right—I've made some rules myself. Rules like the Ten Commandments and others will really help people's lives to be better and happier if they keep them. Now what do you think of rules?*

Sandy: Rule number 1 is this: "Never look down on a rule until you've looked at the reason for its being there." And rule number 2 says, "Keep the rules for your own good."

GOD: *Those are good rules. Keep them and you'll have a happier and safer life.*

Sandy: I plan to make it a rule, Lord.

Questions

1. Do you think rules are important for society? Why? Do you think rules are good for youth?

2. Nearly all youth desire personal freedom. How do rules fit in with freedom? What are some rules you think are unfair? What are some you agree with?

3. What does the term *self-discipline* mean to you? What are some ways you can gain self-discipline? What are some of your own personal rules you use to live by?

4. What are some of God's rules you feel really apply to your life?

Adapted from *event*, February 1977, pages 12-14.

8.
If I'm a Christian, How Come I Feel Lousy?

Bob: Lord, I . . . uh . . . . Lord, I . . . .

GOD: *Don't stumble over your words. Tell me what's bothering you. I'm interested in your needs.*

Bob: I know, but it seems I just keep coming back to you with the same problem over and over again.

GOD: *What problem?*

Bob: Lord, I know you're busy . . . running the universe and all. I'm just one among several billion on earth. I won't take up your time.

GOD: *You see me as a busy executive in the sky.*

Bob: I guess so, in a way. I read somewhere in the Bible that you neither slumber nor sleep. It would be a full-time job taking care of our family, much less the world.

GOD: *You have a lot to learn. Take your Bible and turn to John 4:24.*

Bob: All right. Here it is.

GOD: *Read it out loud.*

Bob: "God is Spirit, and we must have his help to worship as we should."

GOD: *What does it tell you?*

Bob: That you're much more than a busy executive. You're a spirit. You can be with any of us and everywhere at the same time.

GOD: *I'm glad we've settled that for a moment. Now back to the problem you keep stumbling over. Share it with me.*

Bob: OK. Here it is. If I'm a Christian, how come I feel lousy?

GOD: *There's a lot behind that question. Tell me more.*

Bob: Sometimes I feel really good. There are times when I feel happy and close to you.

GOD: *Tell me about one.*

Bob: The last time I remember was the retreat we went on. We had a great time. Lots of fun. You know ol' Buddy?

GOD: *Somewhat.*

Bob: I'm sorry. I forget about how you know everybody. Anyway, we had this "tug-of-war." We had Buddy on our side because he's so big. He's not just fat, but strong.

We had this little hole dug and filled it with water and mud. It was real gooky.

GOD: *"Gooky"?*

Bob: Yeah, sort of slimy and oozy.

GOD: *I see. I'll have to add "gooky" to my word list.*

Bob: Buddy's kind of lazy, so we put him up front. We figured that if he was up front, he'd work harder to keep out of the gook.

GOD: *You had him figured right, did you?*

Bob: Right. When they told us to go, ol' Buddy really started pulling. The kids on the other side started falling into the gook. Buddy was pulling and tugging like a wild man. It looked like we were going to win in a hurry. Buddy was really leaning back on the rope with his heels close to the hole. The kids on the other side just kept on falling in. Wow, what a mess. Buddy suddenly relaxed and stood straight

up. He held the rope with one hand and beat on
his chest with the other. He yelled like Tarzan.
AAAhhh EEEEEAahhh!!

GOD: *I think you'd better hold it down. It's just possible
that someone might wonder if you're praying or going
crazy.*

Bob: I'm sorry. It's just that it's so funny. Just about that
time Ronnie Jackson on the other side jerked the
rope as hard as he could. Buddy lost his balance
and started to fall forward. He started to stutter,
"Oh . . . Oh . . . Oh . . ." And then he fell flat
on his face right in the gook. Splat! Oh, what a
sight! I laughed until I thought I'd just die.

GOD: *What happened to make you feel good on the inside?*

Bob: Later that night we had a campfire. Eddie, our
youth minister, asked the kids to each tell why they
loved the Lord. When it came around to me, I felt
this great sense of love and closeness to you. It was
like a big wave of love came completely over me.
It was a wonderful feeling. When I got home, I
felt good on the inside for a long time, but now
it's gone.

GOD: *Tell me what you think a Christian ought to feel.*

Bob: I'm not sure, Lord, but I think I ought to feel like
that all the time. I mean, if I'm a Christian, I ought
to be happy all the time.

GOD: *Why do you think that?*

  Bob: I've heard that when Christ lives in your life you have all your sins forgiven. Isn't that true?

GOD: *True.*

  Bob: I've heard that when you have Christ in your life you'll have joy. True?

GOD: *True.*

  Bob: Well, right now I'm not joyful.

GOD: *I can tell. Is there someone you think feels happy all the time?*

  Bob: Yes, I think Sandy does. She's always smiling and laughing. She just kind of radiates all the time. Anybody can tell she's a Christian.

GOD: *Sandy was talking to me about her problem recently.*

  Bob: Problem? Sandy? What kind of problem could she have?

GOD: *Do you really want to know?*

  Bob: Sure.

GOD: *She said, "Lord, if I'm a Christian, how come I feel lousy?"*

Bob: Aw, come on, Lord. You wouldn't kid me, would you?

GOD: *Sandy told me it was almost more than she could do to keep up the impression she was always happy. She felt like all the rest of you looked to her and expected her to be happy. The day she spoke to me she cried about it. You see, Bob, you don't know what goes on inside people like I do.*

Bob: If Sandy feels lousy, that makes me feel good . . . I mean terrible . . . Oh, I don't know what I mean.

GOD: *Try to sort it out.*

Bob: I feel good in a way. If Sandy feels bad sometimes, I'm not the only one who feels this way. I feel bad for Sandy. It must be rough trying to pretend to be happy sometimes.

GOD: *Is there a place in the Bible that says you're supposed to feel happy all the time?*

Bob: Hmmm . . . Let me think . . . I don't know your Word all that much. Hmmm . . . I can't think of a single verse that tells me I should feel happy *all* the time.

GOD: *In fact, there are times when you should feel sad.*

Bob: Really? When?

GOD: *Read Luke 19:41-42. See whether or not you think I was always happy.*

Bob: Luke 19. All right. Let's see . . . Here it is. "But as they came closer to Jerusalem and he saw the city ahead, he began to cry. 'Eternal peace was within your reach and you turned it down,' he wept, 'and now it is too late.' "

I see what you mean, Lord. You couldn't be happy when people turned you down. It says right here that you cried.

GOD: *Being spiritual doesn't mean you are always happy.*

Bob: But awhile ago you agreed with me that being spiritual meant to be joyful. I don't think I understand.

GOD: *There's a difference between joy and happiness. Almost anyone can be happy temporarily. Taking a ride on a roller coaster, winning a game, having fun with friends . . . all can make people happy. Joy is an inner quality that makes you think positively even in the midst of hard times.*

Bob: I think I see the difference, Lord, but I'm not feeling lousy for the same reasons you felt sad. I'm not feeling bad because people have turned you down. I'm just depressed and low.

GOD: *It's all right.*

Bob: All right?

GOD: *Yes. It's all right to feel like you do from time to time. You've been under a lot of pressure. Things haven't always gone well for you. You've worked hard, and the results still haven't been the best. Be patient with yourself. Stay close to me.*

Bob: I'm already feeling better. I thought being depressed meant I wasn't a Christian. I was getting more depressed because I was afraid I'd lost you.

GOD: *You'll never lose me.*

Bob: I won't?

GOD: *No. I promised never to leave you or forsake you. I keep my promises.*

Bob: You know, Lord, I don't feel depressed anymore. I'm not happy, especially . . . just not sad.

GOD: *What changed your feelings?*

Bob: Let me think about it for a minute. Hmmm . . . well, first it helped me a lot to find out you weren't always happy. I think I had the idea a Christian would always be "ha-ha happy" if he lived close to you.

GOD: *"Ha-ha happy"?*

Laughing all the time.

GOD: *You have a way with words. "Ha-ha happy" is another I'll add to my word list. What else did you learn?*

Bob: I learned that Sandy didn't always feel the way I thought. I found out she felt the same as I do sometimes. That helped. In fact, she's probably more depressed than me from time to time. She has to fake being happy even when she isn't happy on the inside.

GOD: *Now you're learning. Keep on. What else did you find out?*

Bob: I found out that being joyful and being happy could be two different things. It was "happy" funny when Buddy fell in the gook at the retreat. It was joyful when I felt love for you during the campfire that night.

Something else, Lord. I learned that even in the bad times I could always know you were with me and would give me joy.

GOD: *Now take a look inside. How are you feeling?*

Bob: Not so lousy. Not so good either. Still, I know my relationship with you doesn't depend on whether I'm high or low. You're always with me.

GOD: *You've learned a lot today. In the future, remember that I'm always around, regardless of how you feel. Knowing that will help you get past your depression.*

Bob: Thank you, Lord. I sure am feeling better. I doubt I'll ever feel as lousy again.

Questions

1. What are some experiences that make you happy? Are there some specific Christian experiences that bring you joy?

2. Since Jesus himself did not feel happy at all times, do you think his followers ought to? What are some things that should make us feel concerned rather than happy?

3. What is the difference between joy and happiness? What are some things you can do when you feel low?

The Bible verses quoted are taken from *The Living Bible, Paraphrased* (Wheaton: Tyndale House Publishers, 1971), and are used by permission.

9.
About Those Miracles . . .

Sandy: I don't believe it. I really don't believe it.

GOD: *What is it you don't believe?*

Sandy: Excuse me, Lord, but I have a hard time believing all this stuff about miracles. I'm always hearing about people who claim to have had some miracle happen to them. Later, it seems their so-called miracle wasn't one after all.

GOD: *You have doubts about miracles.*

Sandy: I know I should trust you and believe you have the power to do anything. I heard of someone who took strychnine poison. He did it to prove his faith. Nothing would happen to him, he thought, because he believed you would perform a miracle. But, Lord, he did die.

GOD: *You've probably heard of other such incidents.*

Sandy: Well, yes. I heard about the boy who was supposed

to have been healed of diabetes after going to a faith healer. He wasn't, but his parents refused to give him his medication. They thought it would be a denial of faith.

They waited too long, and the boy died. Even then the parents believed you were going to do a miracle. They claimed their son was going to come back to life again within four days, and it would be an even greater miracle.

He didn't come back to life; and what's more, the faith healer wasn't heard from again either.

GOD: *So you doubt miracles?*

Sandy: I'm sorry, Lord, but yes, I do.

GOD: *I don't blame you.*

Sandy: I really feel bad, like I let you down . . . what did you say?

GOD: *I said, "I don't blame you."*

Sandy: But wait a minute. I thought if I doubted miracles it meant I didn't have enough faith in you. What do you mean, you don't blame me?

GOD: *You will always be wise to carry healthy doubt about miracle workers. There are many foolish people who will believe anything anyone tells them. Sadly, there are also many people who are desperate. They will try anything to get over their suffering.*

Sandy: I'm feeling better, Lord. I thought you'd really be angry with me for doubting about miracles.

GOD: *I didn't say miracles don't happen. I said you would be wise in doubting miracle workers.*

Sandy: I think I get it. It's not that you don't have the power to work miracles. Some have misused the Bible and misunderstood how you work. Is that it?

GOD: *Now you're beginning to understand.*

Sandy: Lord, can I ask some other things? I don't want you to think I doubt you. I really don't, but I haven't seen anything take place as it did in the Bible.

GOD: *Go ahead.*

Sandy: I read where you healed the lepers and all. I don't have the foggiest notion of what leprosy is. I haven't seen anybody with the disease, but it must've been bad.

I have seen blind people. The Bible says you healed a blind man . . . what was his name?

GOD: *You're thinking of Bartimaeus.*

Sandy: Yes. That's the one. How do you know what I'm thinking?

GOD: *It's one of the benefits of being God.*

Sandy: Oh.

GOD: *What about Bartimaeus?*

Sandy: Oh, well, what am I supposed to do with that? He's not around for me to talk with. No modern doctors could confirm whether or not a genuine miracle took place. It happened so long ago.

GOD: *There are some other miracles that bother you, I believe.*

Sandy: I might as well just let it all out. Yes, there are. Lazarus was another story. According to the Bible, he had been dead four days when you arrived at his home. You asked that the stone be removed from the opening of the tomb. One of his sisters tried to stop you. She said, "Lord, he stinketh."

Whooo. That's really bad. She knew he was dead, dead, dead. Then you prayed, and out popped Lazarus.

GOD: *He hardly "popped" out. Lazarus was not a jack-in-the-box.*

Sandy: I didn't mean to be irreverent, but the whole story is spooky to me. If I went to a cemetery and saw some folks digging open a grave while somebody was praying, I'd be scared stiff. I'd probably faint if somebody got up out of a coffin and started walking around after he'd been in there four days.

GOD: *It amazed the people who were there then. Yours is not the only generation that understands about death. When someone died he remained dead. That was the miracle. I intervened in the natural state of events.*

Sandy: I hear what you're saying, but it just doesn't happen anymore. What doesn't happen anymore makes me wonder if it ever happened in the first place. This is the twentieth century, Lord. People aren't as superstitious. What passed off as miracles back then might not have been at all.

GOD: *You are a skeptic, aren't you?*

Sandy: I may as well go ahead and tell you about some other doubts.

GOD: *Feel free.*

Sandy: I've been told all my life about how you were conceived in the virgin Mary. I know it has great meaning to many people, but there's no way anyone could prove it. How could anyone really know that Mary was a virgin?

GOD: *You think you are the only generation with facts.*

But I'll let you in on a little secret.

Sandy: You will?

GOD: *Yes.*

Sandy: What?

GOD: *They knew what made babies back then, too.*

Sandy: Oh, come on, Lord, I've got to believe they must've just made up a good story in order to make your greatness even greater.

GOD: *I see you've got your Bible handy. Turn to Luke 1 and read the story.*

Sandy: OK . . . Hmmmm . . . Luke 1. Here it is.

GOD: *Read verse 34.*

Sandy: "Mary asked the angel, 'But how can I have a baby? I am a virgin.'"

GOD: *Do you think Mary knew how babies were conceived?*

Sandy: It sure sounds like it.

GOD: *Turn back to Matthew 1 and read verses 18-19.*

Sandy: "These are the facts concerning the birth of Jesus

Christ: His mother, Mary, was engaged to be married to Joseph. But while she was still a virgin she became pregnant by the Holy Spirit. Then Joseph, her fiancé, being a man of stern principle, decided to break the engagement but to do it quietly, as he didn't want to publicly disgrace her."

GOD: *What does the passage say to you?*

Sandy: It sounds like Joseph was upset about Mary.

GOD: *Why?*

Sandy: Because virgin women don't get pregnant.

GOD: *Exactly. All of this was to let you know they knew about sex and childbearing. It was just as shocking and surprising to Mary and Joseph as it would be to anyone today.*

Sandy: All right, maybe they did know some facts. Still, I have my doubts.

GOD: *Good. As I said, keep a healthy skepticism about miraculous claims.*

Sandy: Well, I guess that settles that. I doubt miracles. That's the end of that.

GOD: *Not quite.*

Sandy: What do you mean?

GOD: *Would you be open to prove a miracle for yourself?*

Sandy: Me? Prove a miracle?

GOD: *Yes.*

Sandy: What are you going to get me into? Am I going to be able to appear and disappear, fly over a mountain, or heal a kitty cat?

GOD: *Something much better.*

Sandy: I can hardly wait. I really want to see this miracle.

GOD: *You won't "see" it.*

Sandy: Oh, no. Here we go again. I really have a hard time understanding you sometimes, Lord. If I don't see it, how can I know it really happened?

GOD: *You will experience it. Trust me.*

Sandy: All right, I trust you. Tell me about this miracle I'll experience.

GOD: *You know the story about my resurrection from the dead.*

Sandy: Sure.

GOD: *You weren't there to see it.*

Sandy: That's obvious. I don't get your point.

GOD: *There was someone there who had difficulty believ-*
ing in my resurrection. You know him as "Doubting
Thomas."

Sandy: Oh, him. I've always wondered why they called
him "Doubting Thomas."

GOD: *Because he doubted I had come to life again. Some*
of my followers tried to convince Thomas I had risen
from the dead. Find John 20:25-29 and read what
it says.

Sandy: OK. It says, "When they kept telling him, 'We
have seen the Lord,' he replied, 'I won't believe
it unless I see the nail wounds in his hands—and
put my fingers into them—and place my hand into
his side.' "

GOD: *Hmmm . . . Does that sound like anyone you know?*

Sandy: It sounds like me.

GOD: *Just who I had in mind.*

Sandy: Well, I don't blame him, Lord. After all, those
sorts of things don't happen every day. He wanted
some proof.

GOD: *Read on.*

Sandy: All right. "Eight days later the disciples were to-
gether again, and this time Thomas was with them.
The doors were locked; but suddenly, as before,
Jesus was standing among them and greeting them.

"Then he said to Thomas, 'Put your finger into
my hands. Put your hand into my side. Don't be
faithless any longer. Believe!'

" 'My Lord and my God!' Thomas said.

"Then Jesus told him, 'You believe because you
have seen me. But blessed are those who haven't
seen me and believe anyway.' "

GOD: *What does all of that say to you?*

Sandy: It's a really exciting story. It sounds like Thomas
had to have some proof, and you gave it to him.

GOD: *What else?*

Sandy; It says . . . it says. Wait a minute. It just dawned
on me. Thomas had said he wouldn't believe until
he had seen the nail wounds. As far as he knew,
you were nowhere around. You couldn't be seen.

When you came again eight days later you offered
to show Thomas the places where they had put
the nails. It can only mean one thing.

GOD: *What's that?*

Sandy: Why, you were listening to Thomas express his
doubts even though he couldn't see you.

GOD: *Now it's coming through. Go on. I think you're about to grasp the point.*

Sandy: You told Thomas that anyone would be blessed who believed, even if they hadn't seen you. I haven't seen you, so if I believe in you, then I will receive a blessing.

GOD: *And what blessing is that?*

Sandy: It can only mean one thing. The blessing of having you live in my heart. Sure! That's it. That's got to be it. If I believe in you, then you come to live in me. I can experience you inside me. I've already done that.

GOD: *Do you think you had to be in Jerusalem to prove my resurrection?*

Sandy: No. Not at all. Why, everybody can find out for themselves. If they ask you to come into their hearts, then you come alive inside them. The experience proves you got out of the grave alive. A dead person can't come into people's hearts.

GOD: *The Holy Spirit would be the spiritual presence, don't you think?*

Sandy: Oh, I really see now. The greatest miracle of all is the inside job you do on people who believe in you.

GOD: *I'm proud of you. You're really seeing for the first time about miracles. There's one other thing, though.*

Sandy: What's that, Lord?

GOD: *You do accept the fact that I was raised from the dead because my Spirit has entered your heart?*

Sandy: Absolutely.

GOD: *Tell me, do you think if I could be raised from the dead and then change people's lives from within, I could do those other miracles you've wondered about?*

Sandy: Hmmmm . . . I hadn't thought about it like that, but sure. If you can do the greatest miracle of all, those others would be a piece of cake to you.

GOD: *I don't think I would call it a "piece of cake," but yes—if I can do the greatest miracle, I can do the others as well.*

Sandy: You know what I feel like saying?

GOD: *Tell me.*

Sandy: I feel like saying what Thomas did.

GOD: *Go ahead.*

Sandy: Jesus, you're my Lord and my God.

Questions

1. We hear a lot about miracles these days. What really is a miracle? Define the term as you understand it.

2. Take a few moments to read John 9. If something like that happened today, do you think you would believe it? Why?

3. What is the difference between Jesus and the so-called miracle workers of our day?

4. Do you believe miracles still happen? If so, in what ways? According to your definition of a miracle, could you share such an experience with others?

5. What is the greatest miracle of all?

6. Has it happened to you?

The Bible verses quoted are taken from *The Living Bible, Paraphrased* (Wheaton: Tyndale House Publishers, 1971), and are used by permission.

10.
When Bob "Wised Up"

Bob: OK, this is it. I really feel good about this test, Lord. Even though I didn't study for it, I know you'll help me make a good grade. Yes sir, I'm doing what they've been talking about . . . I've surrendered my whole self to you. I'm letting you take over. I just thank you ahead of time for the answer I know I'm going to get.

GOD: *You're thanking me ahead of time, are you?*

Bob: Why, yes, Lord. It's wonderful being a Christian. I know you'll take over and help me do things I couldn't have done without you.

GOD: *You'd better wait until you get your test grade before you thank me.*

Bob: Wait a minute . . . . oh, whew. For a moment there I had the feeling you weren't going to help me do good on the test.

You are going to help me on the test, even though

I didn't study, aren't you?

Lord, Lord? . . . Lord! Don't let me down now. Oh, please don't let me down.

GOD: *I'm not going to help you "remember" something you never knew in the first place. That's not what "surrendering" to me means. If you don't do well on the test, it won't be because I let you down. It will be because you let yourself down. That was a bad choice on your part . . . deciding not to study.*

Bob: But they tell me if I just turn my whole life over to you, then everything'll be all right. That's what I'm doing.

GOD: *Bob, what you mean is that you decided to turn everything over to me after it was too late to study. If you had done that earlier and studied along with it, everything would have been all right.*

Bob: Oh, man, am I in trouble. I was really counting on you, Lord. I mean, this is going to be one of those make-or-break tests, you know?

GOD: *I know. You knew it before now, too.*

Bob: OK, I can see what you're saying. Surrendering to you means I'm still responsible for decisions. I can't blame you if I don't do well.

Boy, oh boy, what am I going to do? I'm scared to death now. What'll my parents think when I get this bad grade? Man, I won't get to go out for two weeks.

GOD: *I will do something for you.*

Bob: Anything! Oh . . . anything.

GOD: *I'll help you remember what you do know. Too, I'll help you to be as calm as possible. But remember, Bob, prayer won't make up for ignorance.*

Bob: Lord, I'm really low. I haven't been this low in a long time. I sure don't want to get in this shape anymore. How can I keep from getting in this mess again?

GOD: *Later, Bob, later. There's a time for prayer, and there's a time to work. Right now you have twenty-two minutes to get ready for that test. Use the time to get ready as best you can.*

(One week later, Bob walks dejectedly into his bedroom.)

GOD: *What have you got in your hand?*

Bob: My test from last week.

GOD: *Why do you have it folded like that?*

Bob: I don't want you to see what I made.

GOD: Don't worry.

Bob: What do you mean?

GOD: I saw your teacher grade it.

Bob: Oh.

GOD: What are you thinking? Go ahead and say it.

Bob: Well, first of all, I got through by the skin of my teeth. You know those last twenty-two minutes?

GOD: Yes.

Bob: If I hadn't used the time like you said, I would've flunked it so badly I probably would've failed the whole course.

It's bad enough as it is. Lord, my parents will really be upset, but I want you to know I'm grateful. It could've been worse.

You know, when I think about it, I make a lot of bad choices.

GOD: I've noticed.

Bob: Why is it that I get into such messes all the time?

GOD: You have an occasion in mind?

Bob: You remember last Monday night when I should've

been home studying?

GOD: *I remember. What about it?*

Bob: I went out with Roger that night. I told my parents I was going to his house and study for the exam. Instead, we drove around and wound up in a pizza place.

When it got late, Mom started worrying about me. She's like that, you know.

GOD: *I know.*

Bob: She called Roger's folks. His parents don't keep up with what he's doing as much as mine do me. They told Mom we'd been gone for a long time.

Well, when we got home, my mother was all upset. My dad stood there in the hall with a big frown on his face. "Where in the world have you been?" they asked.

I had to think quick, so I lied. "Roger's car broke down."

GOD: *That's an old line. Not only was it a lie; it was a bad lie at that.*

Bob: They caught me at it. My mom was standing real close to me. She had tears in her eyes. She looked me right in the face and said, "That's not the truth, and you know it. You've been eating pizza. You haven't been studying like you said."

Lord, how did she know that?

GOD: *You said your mother was standing close to you?*

Bob: Yes.

GOD: *Pepperoni pizza breath is hard to disguise.*

Bob: Oh, that's how she knew.

GOD: *Yes,* oh. *How about making some wise choices in the future?*

Bob: I'm for that. Where do I start?

GOD: *Turn to James 1:5-8 in my Word.*

Bob: OK. Let's see. Here it is: "If you want to know what God wants you to do, ask him, and he will gladly tell you, for he is always ready to give a bountiful supply of wisdom to all who ask him; he will not resent it. But when you ask him, be sure that you really expect him to tell you, for a doubtful mind will be as unsettled as a wave of the sea that is driven and tossed by the wind; and every decision you then make will be uncertain, as you turn first this way, and then that. If you don't ask with faith, don't expect the Lord to give you any solid answer."

GOD: *What do you think?*

Bob: That's a wonderful promise. It means you'll help me make wise choices if I trust you and talk to you about it ahead of time.

GOD: *Now you're getting someplace. Will I make all your decisions for you?*

Bob: No. I'm responsible for my decisions.

GOD: *Will you have to make your decisions alone?*

Bob: No. You'll help me.

GOD: *There now. You've got it down. You see what it takes to make wise decisions with my help. It's time to get started right now.*

Bob: What do you mean?

GOD: *Take that folded test paper. Go to your mother. Admit what you did. Apologize and promise to do better.*

Bob: OK, but it'll be hard.

GOD: *Not nearly as hard as what you've been through already.*

Bob: That's true. All right, Lord. Here goes.

GOD: *Congratulations.*

Bob: For what?

GOD: *For making a good, wise choice. Who knows, you might grow up to be a "wise guy" one day.*

Bob: Thanks a lot. You know, Lord, I really hope you're right, in the best sense of that word.

GOD: *That's how I meant it. If you'll stay close to me, it can happen. I'm looking forward to it.*

Questions

1. What does the word *wise* mean to you? Do you know some people you think are wise? Think about them for a moment. What makes them wise?

2. Everyone makes mistakes. When you make mistakes, do you repeat them or learn from them?

3. Find James 1:5-8 in your Bible. What is God's method of gaining wisdom?

4. What are some things you could begin doing that would make you wiser?

Adapted from *event,* October 1976, pages 17-21. The Bible verses quoted are taken from *The Living Bible, Paraphrased* (Wheaton: Tyndale House Publishers, 1971), and are used by permission.

11.
I Never Thought of It
That Way Before

Bob: Lord, I guess I've sinned.

GOD: *What do you mean, "guess"?*

Bob: Well, there are times when I'm not serious. I tend
to laugh a lot, especially when something's really
funny. I really like to have a good time. Later, when
I think how serious a good Christian is supposed
to be—well, I feel guilty about having a good time.
That's what I mean about guessing I've sinned.

GOD: *Tell me about a good time you had.*

Bob: You remember the youth retreat we had last week-
end?

GOD: *Yes, I was there.*

Bob: Oh, I keep forgetting.

GOD: *I've noticed. Go on with your story.*

Bob: Troy is a pretty good guy. All of us like him. But you know him; he's always picking on the smaller guys and bragging about how tough he is. He's funny a lot of times, too.

When he sleeps, he really sleeps. He just goes completely unconscious. The trouble is, he's the last one to go to sleep. He keeps the rest of us awake joking around.

He's almost impossible to wake up. When it was time to get up the next morning, he was still asleep in the bunk above me. I whispered to Jimmy, "Hey, Jimmy, you ready?" He giggled. "Yeah," he said.

We both got up and got some shaving cream . . . you know, the kind in a can?

GOD: *I know. Go on. What happened next?*

Bob: Well, we sprayed a heaping handful in his right hand. He never felt it. We had to climb down from his bunk several times, we were laughing so hard. Finally, I got control enough to go back. I'd found this bird feather the night before . . . that's what gave me the idea. I took the feather and tickled the end of his nose.

He kind of crinkled his nose but didn't do anything. I tickled it again. This time I ran it all the way up and down the side of his nose. He shook his head. All the other guys were watching and nearly burst with laughter.

The next time, I put the feather on his right cheek and moved it along like it might be a fly. I pulled it right up to the tip of his nose and tickled it real fast.

Suddenly . . . SPLAT! He hit his nose with that handful of shaving cream! The stuff went all over his face. It got in his hair and eyebrows. He sat straight up in bed. He opened his mouth, and some of it fell in.

He sputtered and spit. I literally rolled on the floor laughing. So did a lot of the guys.

GOD: *I did, too.*

Bob: Even Troy thought it was funny when he realized what had happened. He laughed, and we all had a good time over it. I bet he'll get me back, though. Anyway, later I kind of felt bad about it. People keep telling me how serious a Christian is always supposed to be.

Wait a minute. What did you say last time?

GOD: *I did, too.*

Bob: You "did too" what?

GOD: *Laugh.*

Bob: You laughed? At the joke I pulled?

GOD: *I was there, you know. But I wanted you to tell me about it. I enjoy the way you tell things. You do have a flair for the dramatic.*

Bob: I don't get it. I never thought about you enjoying anything except the serious stuff. I've heard people say things like, "The Bible never tells us that Jesus laughed. He was a man of a broken heart. He was a man full of sorrows over the sins of the world."

GOD: *That's partly true.*

Bob: What part?

GOD: *I am deeply concerned over the sins of the world. Sometimes my heart does break when men sin and damage one another. If it had not been for my concern over the sins of men, I would never have had the cross to bear.*

Bob: What about the other side?

GOD: *It's true that the Bible never talks about me laughing. But look at it from another standpoint. What kind of news does your newspaper report?*

Bob: Bad news?

GOD: *Not necessarily. Just the unusual news. The papers don't tell about people going to church. That's not unusual. But let a church building catch on fire . . . that's news, and the papers carry pictures of it the next day.*

Bob: I understand, but what's that got to do with your sense of humor?

GOD: *The men who wrote my Word told what seemed outstanding things to them. They wanted people to see that the Son of God was compassionate and concerned. They wanted people to read how powerful he was.*

Bob: Wait, I think I'm getting it! The reason the Bible doesn't talk about you laughing or smiling is because that was so common!

GOD: *Now you're beginning to see.*

Bob: I never thought of it that way before.

GOD: *There are a lot of things you've never thought about. Here's something else you missed. The Bible does tell about some good times.*

Bob: It does? Where?

GOD: *Do you remember my first miracle?*

Bob: Let's see. Hmmm. I went to a wedding the other night and I heard the preeacher say something about . . . oh, yeah. Now I remember. You made water into wine.

GOD: Where was I?

Bob: At a wedding feast?

GOD: You would call it a party.

Bob: Hey, that's great! I never thought of it that way before.

GOD: You've already said that. Ready for something else?

Bob: Sure. This is good.

GOD: Thank you.

That's all I do.

You probably remember the Pharisees. They were very serious about their religion. They never laughed or smiled. Too, they didn't want anyone else to enjoy their faith. One day I'd had enough of their criticisms. Want to read about it?

Bob: Do I! Where's it found?

GOD: Turn to Matthew 11:16-19. When you've found it, read it out loud.

Bob: Hmmm . . . here it is. "What shall I say about this nation? These people are like children playing, who say to their little friends, 'We played wedding and you weren't happy, so we played funeral but you weren't sad.' For John the Baptist doesn't even drink wine and often goes without food, and you say, 'He's crazy.' And, I, the Messiah, feast and drink, and you complain that I am a glutton and a drinking man, and hang around with the worst sort of sinners! But brilliant men like you can justify your every inconsistency!"

GOD: *What does that sound like to you?*

Bob: It sounds like you were being critized for having a good time with people who the so-called "religious folk" didn't like. I never thought of it that way before.

GOD: *So you've said . . . so you've said. Another thing. I told jokes, too.*

Bob: Jokes? You?

GOD: *That's right. You probably missed them, though. You see, when you read the Bible with only one thought in mind, you miss anything else.*

Want to read one?

Bob: I sure do. Where's it found?

GOD: *You'll find one in Matthew 7:3-4.*

Bob: OK. All right, here it is. "And why worry about a speck in the eye of a brother when you have a board in your own? Should you say, 'Friend, let

me help you get that speck out of your eye,' when
you can't even see because of the board in your
own?"

Hey, that's pretty good, Lord. I never thought of
it that way before.

GOD: *I know. I know. Now that you have thought of it
that way, what do you think about having a good
time?*

Bob: I think you want us to express our humor and enjoy
a good time because we belong to you.

GOD: *Now you're coming along. When you're happy with
other Christians and laugh a lot, I'm right there with
you. I enjoy a good time, too.*

Bob: I never thought of it that way before.

GOD: *You might try thinking every now and then. You'll
discover a lot of great things in my Word if you do.*

Bob: I never . . .

GOD: *I know. You never thought of it that way before.*

Questions

1. What are some reasons that Christians can have good times?

2. Close your eyes and think of Jesus. Picture him in your imagination. What does he look like to you? Does he have a smile on his face? Is he frowning? If you could put your picture of Christ on canvas, would others be drawn to him or would the picture make them believe Jesus was angry?

3. Does Christ approve of good times? Is there a kind of "fun" he doesn't approve? What are the right and wrong kinds of good times for Christians to be involved with?

Adapted from *event*, June 1976, pages 8-11. The Bible verses quoted are taken from *The Living Bible, Paraphrased* (Wheaton: Tyndale House Publishers, 1971), and are used by permission.

12.
"Lord, I Really Love You"

(Bob is humming a happy tune as he takes a shower. He gets louder and louder and finally breaks out in song. His singing leaves something to be desired.)

GOD: *You sound happy.*

Bob: What?

GOD: *You sound happy.*

Bob: Who's there? It's too loud in here for me to hear.

GOD: *Maybe if you didn't make so much noise . . .*

Bob: What? I can't hear you.

(God's voice booms through the room, rattling the windows.)

GOD: *Can you hear me now?*

128

Bob: Oh, it must be you, Lord.

GOD: *Were you expecting someone else while you were in the shower?*

Bob: No, I just didn't expect you. I don't think of the shower as a place of prayer.

GOD: *Keep in mind that I'm everywhere.*

Bob: Even in the shower?

GOD: *Even there.*

Bob: Well, wait a minute, Lord. Let me get out of here. I want to talk to you. Even if you're with me in the shower, I can't think as well. I don't think I can get used to praying while I'm in here.

(Bob comes out of the bathroom, drying his hair with a towel. He has put on jeans and a T-shirt.)

Bob: Lord, I want to say straight out, I love you.

GOD: *Thank you, Bob. What's caused this sudden surge of joy and praise?*

Bob: I was going over all the good things that are mine because of you. When I did, it just made me happy. I know I'm always asking for things and complaining about stuff. I'll probably do some more. Just now, though, I want to praise you and tell you how much I love you.

GOD: *What things bring out your joy?*

Bob: I was reading my Bible the other day. James wrote some beautiful thoughts. The Bible says, "But whatever is good and perfect comes to us from God, the Creator of all light, and he shines forever without change or shadow. And it was a happy day for him when he gave us our new lives, through the truth of his Word, and we became as it were, the first children in his new family" (Jas. 1:17-18).

GOD: *Reading that stirred some thinking.*

Bob: It really did. I got to thinking about all the good things, like just being alive. I'm glad to be alive. I like living.

GOD: *I've noticed.*

Bob: And the food I eat every day. I like to eat, Lord.

GOD: *Others have noticed.*

Bob: My dad's always complaining about how much I eat. He says that my stomach's a bottomless pit or that I have a hollow leg. He claims nobody's natural-sized stomach can hold all the stuff I cram in.

GOD: *You do stretch the boundaries of my creation.*

Bob: Anyway, I'm thankful for food . . . any kind of

food. Well, almost any kind of food. I could get along without asparagus and prunes and spinach. Why did you make stuff like that, anyway?

GOD: Into each life some asparagus must fall.

Bob: If you're trying to tell me that eating asparagus makes me appreciate French fries, you're right. Back to what I was saying, though . . . I'm really thankful for food.

GOD: Is there more?

Bob: Much more. I know I gripe a lot about my folks, but I'm really thankful for them, too. I don't often think about it, but my dad works hard. Sometimes he has some rough days. Still, he doesn't complain too much. I've heard him say over and over how glad he is to have a good job so he can support us. He really is a great dad . . . well, most of the time.

GOD: And your mother?

Bob: Oh, well, she's tops . . . the number 1 mom of the universe as far as I'm concerned. We don't always get along; but when I really think hard about it, why, she has to be the best around. I know Randy and I drive her up the wall sometimes, but she loves us through it all.

GOD: And Randy?

Bob: What about him?

GOD: *Are you thankful for him?*

Bob: Moving right along, Lord. I'm thankful for the ol' car I drive and . . .

GOD: *What about Randy?*

Bob: Lord, I'm feeling really good. I'm making my list of things for which I'm thankful. If I'm going to be honest, I can't say that Randy's on my list right now.

GOD: *All right. What are some other things for which you're honestly thankful?*

Bob: I'm honestly thankful for my friends. More and more lately, I've realized how important they are. Not long ago I was really low. I lay on my bed and felt sorry for myself. It suddenly came to me why. I felt neglected by my friends for a few days.

Just yesterday I had a great time with my friends. That's probably why I'm happier today.

GOD: *Friends are very important.*

Bob: I don't want you to think I'm thankful only for things like food and clothes and stuff. I'm thankful for people. Most of all, though, I'm thankful for spiritual joy. I've been reading your Word more lately. Suddenly, it seems like you've spoken to me directly each time. My joy has been getting greater and greater. I love the Bible more than ever before.

GOD: *You've discovered how I speak through the Bible. By doing so, you've found one of the greatest spiritual secrets of all time. You'll never be far from me if you allow me to speak to you from my Word.*

Bob: I like to pray now, too. I used to say "The Lord's Prayer" every day just to get a duty done.

GOD: *I know. That's how this special relationship between us began.*

Bob: I remember. You've taught me so much since. Each time we talk together, I learn more about you and about myself. My whole life has been changed because of prayer. So, for all those reasons and many more, I had to say, "I love you."

GOD: *I believe you. Would you say your spirit matches Matthew 22:37?*

Bob: Matthew 22:37. Hmmm . . . what is that one? Let me see. Here it is. "Love the Lord your God with all your heart, soul, and mind." Yes, Lord, I'd say that's exactly how I feel right now.

GOD: *How about verse 39?*

Bob: Verse 39? "Love your neighbor as much as you love yourself"? Yes, I love the next-door neighbors.

I can't think of any reason not to love the Bakers and the McClures or any of the others.

GOD: What about Randy?

Bob: Randy? He isn't a neighbor. He's my brother.

GOD: A neighbor is anyone with needs.

Bob: Randy has needs, all right. He has a need sometimes for a fist in the mouth.

GOD: If you love me, you'll prove it by loving Randy.

Bob: Lord, I don't have any problem loving you. You've always been good to me. You've always been there when I needed you.

Randy's given me nothing but trouble. He may be my little brother all right, but he's my biggest trouble most of the time.

GOD: "Love me" is more than words.

Bob: I do more than words. I go to church. I give an offering.

GOD: Loving me is more than fulfilling religious duties. Bob, do you really love me?

Bob: Yes, Lord. I love you. I really do. Hey . . . wait a minute. It seems like I remember you asking someone else that question. Now, who was that?

GOD: *You're thinking of Simon Peter.*

Bob: Right. . . . Oh, excuse me, Lord. I know you're always right.

GOD: *Do you remember what I said to Peter after he assured me of his love?*

Bob: Let me think . . . yes, I do. You said, "Then feed my sheep."

GOD: *It still applies.*

Bob: I'll be glad to feed your sheep. What farm are they on? Just leave Randy out of this.

GOD: *Randy is part of my sheepfold. My sheep are people.*

Bob: *(Sigh.)* Well, Lord, I'll tell you this. I love you more than I need to hold grudges against my little brother. I haven't spoken to him for three days. It's time to break the ice. OK. If Randy is a "neighbor and a sheep," then I'll make every effort to love him.

GOD: *Good, Bob. Now I know you genuinely love me.*

Bob: About Randy, Lord.

GOD: *Yes?*

Bob: I'm going to need lots of help in loving him.

GOD: I'll give you the help you need.

Bob: Lord, I've just got to say it again. I know my actions will prove it, but still, I need to say it.

GOD: Go ahead.

Bob: Lord, I really love you.

Questions

1. How do you feel when you're happy? Is there a difference between being happy while having fun and being spiritually happy? When you feel spiritually happy, what are some of the causes?

2. Loving God is important for every Christian. Do you tend to fear God or love him?

3. What are some ways to express love for God?

4. What are some ways you can express your love for God?

5. If you have some "Randys" in your life, think about them. Would you be willing to express your love for God by doing something good for them?